GENERATIONS

A CELEBRATION OF OUR FAMILY

ARTWORK BY KEITH MALLETT

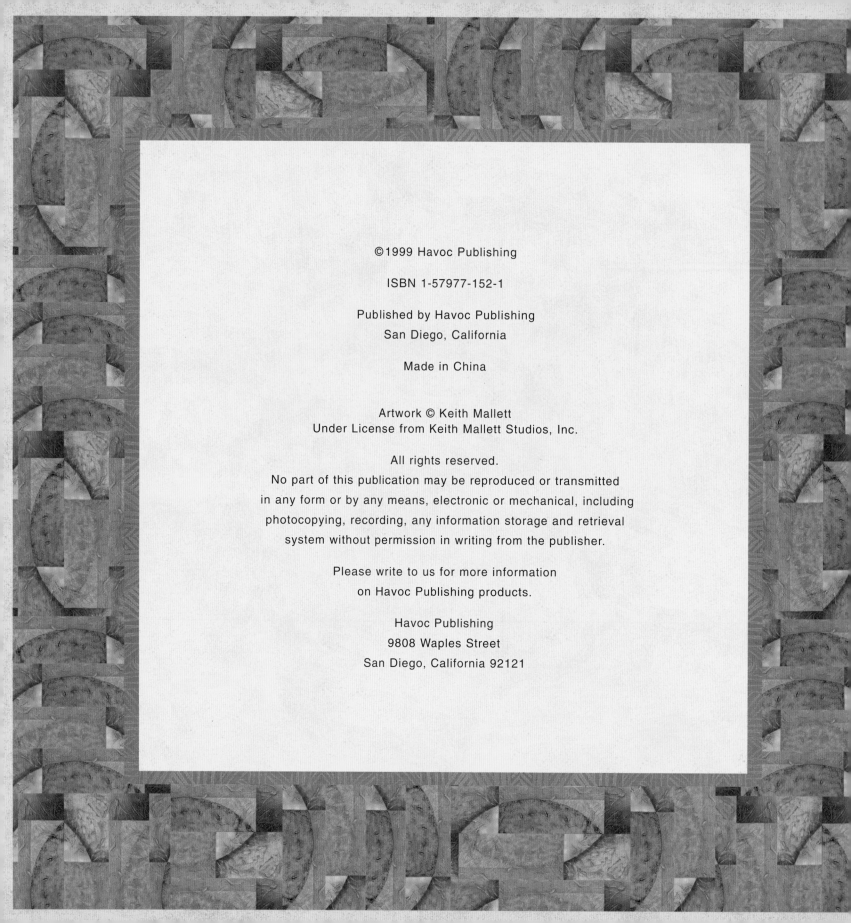

THIS BOOK BELONGS TO:

Karina Hill

TO FORGET ONES ANCESTORS IS
TO BE A BROOK WITHOUT A SOURCE,
A TREE WITHOUT A ROOT - PROVERB

CONTENTS

CONTENTS

OUR FAMILY TREE

GREAT GRANDPARENTS
(FATHER'S SIDE)

GREAT GRANDPARENTS

GRANDFATHER

GRANDMOTHER

FATHER

GREAT GRANDPARENTS
(MOTHER'S SIDE)

GREAT GRANDPARENTS

GRANDFATHER

GRANDMOTHER

MOTHER

CHILDREN

AUNTS

UNCLES

AUNTS

UNCLES

COUSINS

THE FRUIT MUST HAVE A STEM BEFORE IT GROWS. - JABO PROVERB

Great Grandparents
(FATHER'S FATHER'S FAMILY)

MY GREAT GRANDFATHER'S FULL NAME IS _____

_____

THIS IS THE DATE HE WAS BORN _____

I'VE BEEN TOLD MY GREAT GRANDFATHER LIVED HERE _____

_____

THESE ARE SOME OF THE JOBS THAT MY GREAT GRANDFATHER HELD

_____

_____

THIS IS MY GREAT GRANDMOTHER'S FULL NAME _____

_____

MY GREAT GRANDMOTHER WAS BORN _____ AND

SHE GREW UP IN _____

SOME OF THE JOBS MY GREAT GRANDMOTHER HELD ARE _____

_____

MY FAVORITE STORY ABOUT MY GREAT GRANDPARENTS _____

_____

Great Grandparents
(FATHER'S MOTHER'S FAMILY)

MY GREAT GRANDFATHER'S FULL NAME IS _____

_____

THIS IS THE DATE HE WAS BORN _____

I'VE BEEN TOLD MY GREAT GRANDFATHER LIVED HERE _____

_____

THESE ARE SOME OF THE JOBS THAT MY GREAT GRANDFATHER HELD _____

_____

_____

THIS IS MY GREAT GRANDMOTHER'S FULL NAME _____

_____

MY GREAT GRANDMOTHER WAS BORN ON _____ AND

SHE GREW UP IN _____

SOME OF THE JOBS MY GREAT GRANDMOTHER HELD ARE _____

_____

MY FAVORITE STORY ABOUT MY GREAT GRANDPARENTS _____

_____

THIS IS MY GRANDFATHER
(FATHER'S FAMILY)

THIS IS MY GRANDFATHER'S FULL NAME

_____

THIS WAS THE SPECIAL DAY THAT HE WAS BORN

MY GRANDFATHER GREW UP IN

HE TOLD ME THAT HE WENT TO SCHOOL IN

_____

MY FATHER TOLD ME THAT SOME OF HIS SPECIAL INTERESTS AND

HOBBIES WERE

_____

_____

MY FAVORITE STORY ABOUT MY GRANDFATHER IS

_____

_____

_____

THIS IS MY GRANDMOTHER
(FATHER'S FAMILY)

THIS IS MY GRANDMOTHER'S FULL NAME

_____

THIS WAS THE SPECIAL DAY THAT SHE WAS BORN

MY GRANDMOTHER GREW UP IN

SHE TOLD ME THAT SHE WENT TO SCHOOL IN

_____

MY FATHER TOLD ME THAT SOME OF HER SPECIAL INTERESTS AND

HOBBIES WERE

_____

_____

_____

MY FAVORITE STORY ABOUT MY GRANDMOTHER IS

_____

_____

_____

PHOTOGRAPH

PHOTOGRAPH

My Special Father

MY FATHER'S FULL NAME IS _____

NICKNAMES THAT I HAVE FOR MY DAD ARE _____

_____

MY FATHER WAS BORN ON _____

WHEN MY FATHER WAS LITTLE, HE GREW UP IN _____

_____

MY FATHER TOLD ME THAT HE WORKED AT _____

_____

_____

MY FATHER'S FAVORITE HOBBIES ARE _____

_____

_____

ONE THING MY FATHER REMEMBERS MOST ABOUT ME IS _____

_____

_____

_____

_____

AUNTS, UNCLES & COUSINS
(FATHER'S FAMILY)

NAME	RELATION	WHERE THEY LIVE

Great Grandparents
(MOTHER'S FATHER'S FAMILY)

MY GREAT GRANDFATHER'S FULL NAME IS _____

_____

HE WAS BORN ON _____

I'VE BEEN TOLD MY GREAT GRANDFATHER LIVED HERE _____

_____

THESE ARE SOME OF THE JOBS THAT MY GREAT GRANDFATHER HELD

_____

_____

THIS IS MY GREAT GRANDMOTHER'S FULL NAME _____

_____

MY GREAT GRANDMOTHER WAS BORN IN _____ AND

SHE GREW UP IN _____

SOME OF THE JOBS MY GREAT GRANDMOTHER HELD ARE _____

_____

MY FAVORITE STORY ABOUT MY GREAT GRANDPARENTS _____

_____

Great Grandparents
MOTHER'S MOTHER'S FAMILY)

MY GREAT GRANDFATHER'S FULL NAME IS _____

_____

HE WAS BORN ON _____

I'VE BEEN TOLD MY GREAT GRANDFATHER LIVED HERE _____

_____

THESE ARE SOME OF THE JOBS THAT MY GRANDFATHER HELD _____

_____

_____

THIS IS MY GREAT GRANDMOTHER'S FULL NAME _____

_____

MY GREAT GRANDMOTHER WAS BORN ON _____ AND

SHE GREW UP IN _____

SOME OF THE JOBS MY GREAT GRANDMOTHER HELD ARE _____

_____

MY FAVORITE STORY ABOUT MY GREAT GRANDPARENTS _____

_____

THIS IS MY GRANDFATHER
(MOTHER'S FAMILY)

MY GRANDFATHER'S FULL NAME IS _____

_____

THIS WAS THE SPECIAL DAY THAT HE WAS BORN _____

MY GRANDFATHER GREW UP IN _____

HE TOLD ME THAT HE WENT TO SCHOOL IN _____

_____

MY FATHER TOLD ME THAT SOME OF HIS SPECIAL INTERESTS AND

HOBBIES WERE _____

_____

_____

_____

MY FAVORITE STORY ABOUT MY GRANDFATHER IS _____

_____

_____

_____

_____

This is My Grandmother
(MOTHER'S FAMILY)

THIS IS MY GRANDMOTHER'S FULL NAME IS _____

_____

THIS WAS THE SPECIAL DAY THAT HE WAS BORN _____

MY GRANDMOTHER GREW UP IN _____

HE TOLD ME THAT HE WENT TO SCHOOL IN _____

_____

MY FATHER TOLD ME THAT SOME OF HER SPECIAL INTERESTS AND

HOBBIES WERE _____

_____

_____

_____

MY FAVORITE STORY ABOUT MY GRANDMOTHER IS _____

_____

_____

_____

_____

My Special Mother

MY MOTHER'S FULL NAME IS _____

NICKNAMES THAT I HAVE FOR MY MOM ARE _____
_____

MY MOTHER WAS BORN ON _____

WHEN MY MOTHER WAS LITTLE, SHE GREW UP IN _____
_____

MY MOTHER TOLD ME THAT SHE WORKED AT _____
_____
_____
_____

MY MOTHER'S FAVORITE HOBBIES WERE _____
_____
_____
_____

MY FAVORITE STORY ABOUT TIME SPENT WITH MY MOM IS _____
_____
_____
_____
_____

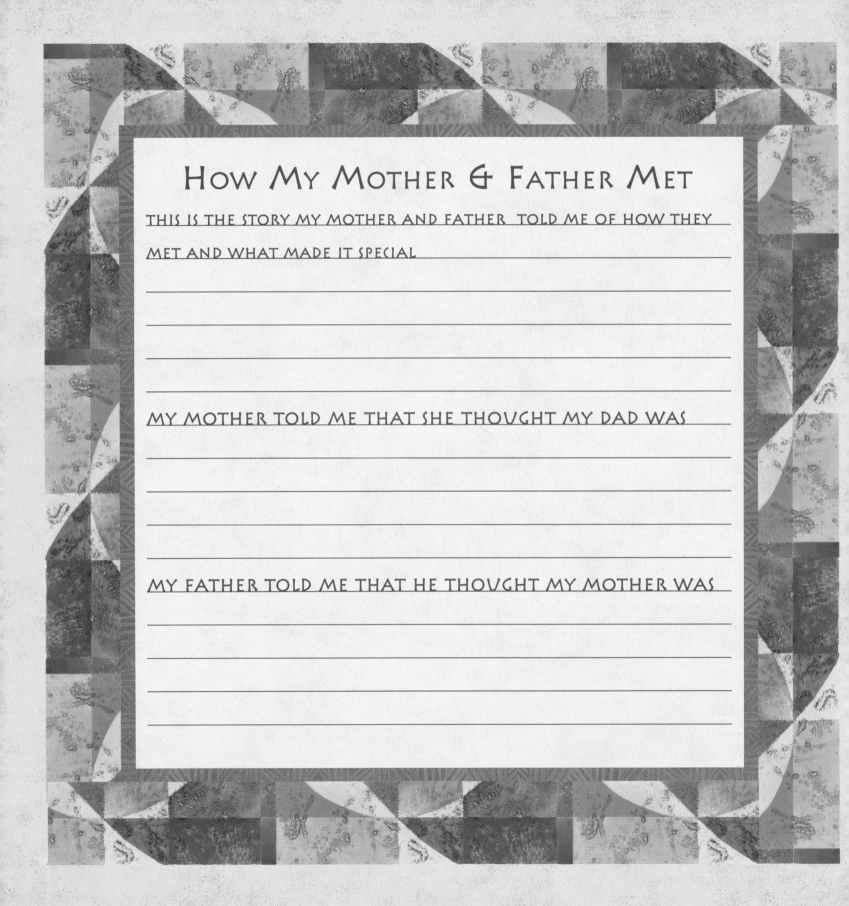

How My Mother & Father Met

THIS IS THE STORY MY MOTHER AND FATHER TOLD ME OF HOW THEY
MET AND WHAT MADE IT SPECIAL

_____

_____

_____

_____

MY MOTHER TOLD ME THAT SHE THOUGHT MY DAD WAS

_____

_____

_____

_____

MY FATHER TOLD ME THAT HE THOUGHT MY MOTHER WAS

_____

_____

_____

_____

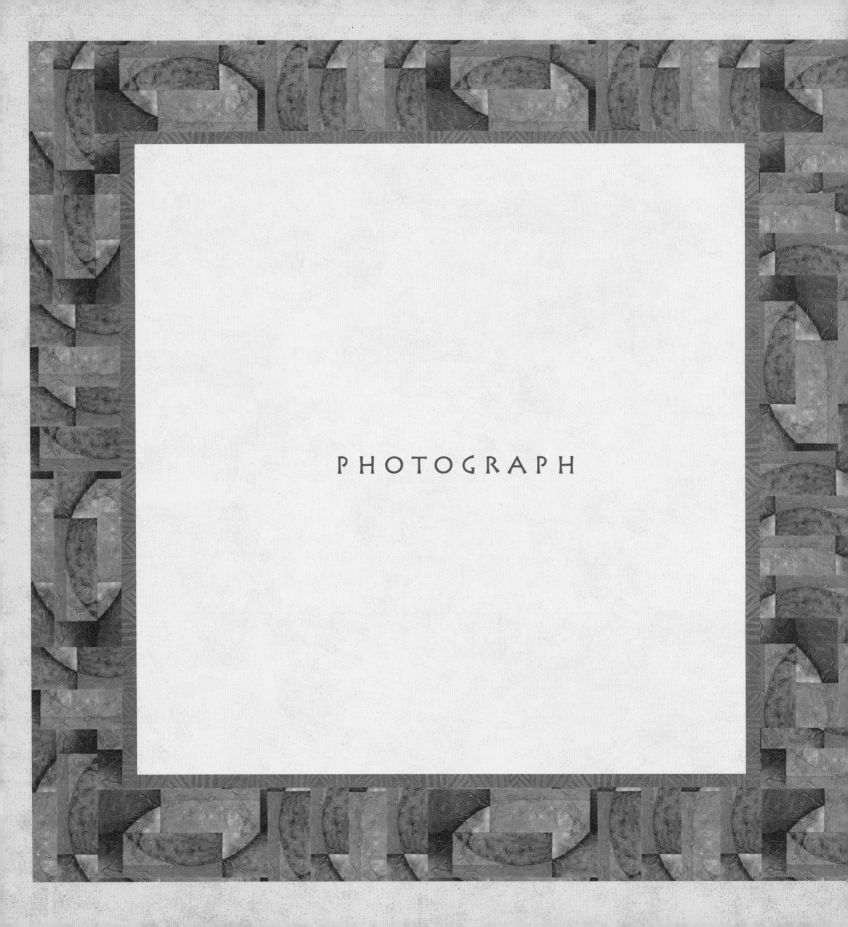

PHOTOGRAPH

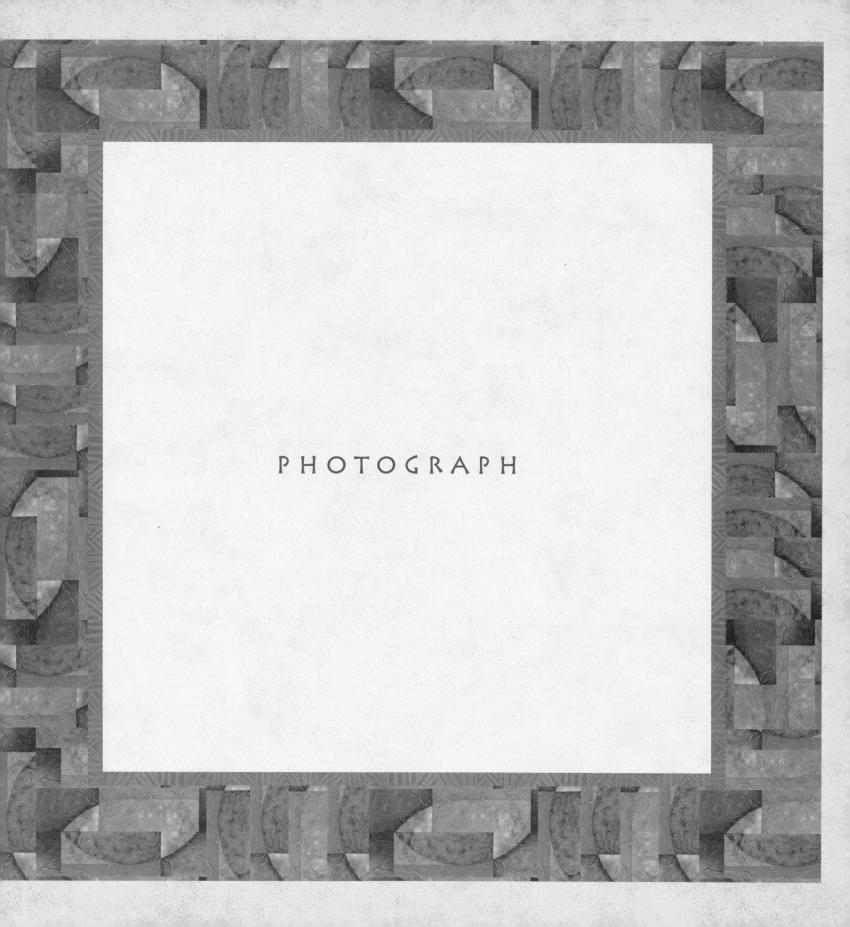

PHOTOGRAPH

Aunts, Uncles & Cousins
(MOTHER'S FAMILY)

NAME	RELATION	WHERE THEY LIVE

Children Are Special People

MY BROTHERS, SISTERS AND COUSINS

_____
_____
_____
_____
_____
_____

THEY ARE ALL UNIQUE IN THEIR OWN SPECIAL WAY

_____
_____
_____
_____
_____
_____

WE DO NOT LIVE FOR OURSELVES ONLY, BUT FOR OUR WIVES AND CHILDREN,
WHO ARE AS DEAR TO US AS THOSE OF ANY OTHER MEN. ~ ABRAHAM

MY FRIENDS ARE FAMILY

MY FRIENDS THAT ARE PART OF THE FAMILY

_____

_____

_____

_____

_____

_____

A LITTLE STORY ABOUT HOW WE MET EACH OTHER

_____

_____

_____

_____

_____

_____

_____

_____

_____

HAVE FRIENDS WRITE A LITTLE SOMETHING HERE

PHOTOGRAPH
WITH FRIENDS

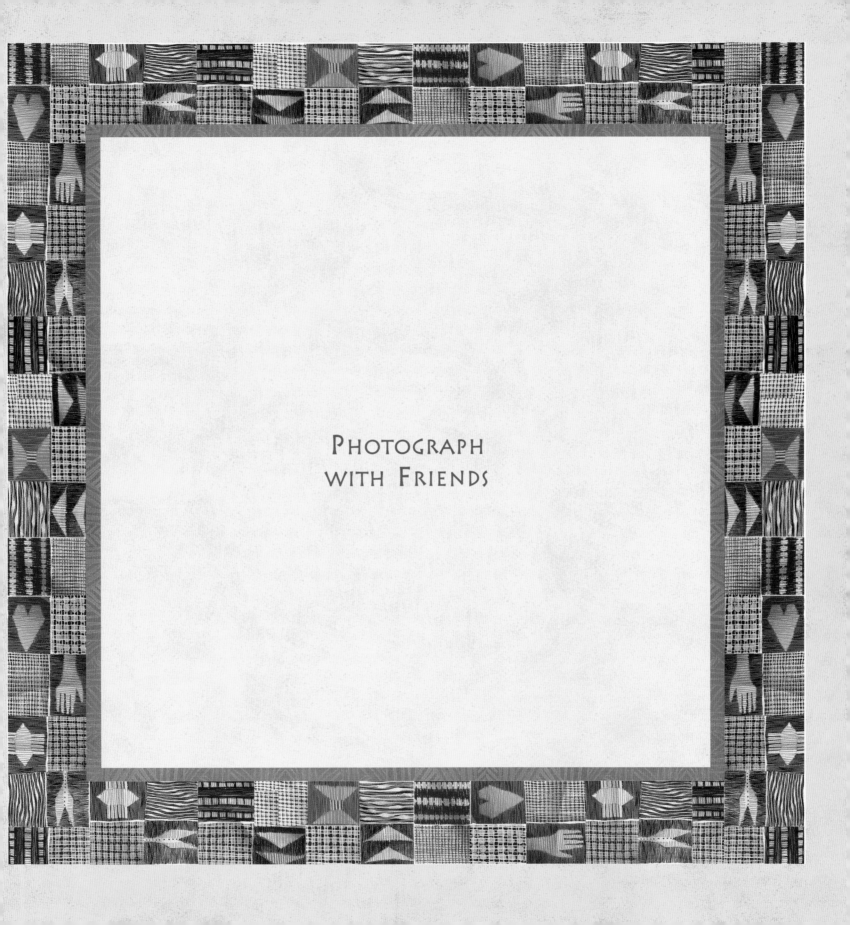

PHOTOGRAPH
WITH FRIENDS

SPRINGTIME MEMORIES

MY FAVORITE CELEBRATIONS ARE
_____
_____
_____
_____
_____
_____
_____

MY FAVORITE SPRING TRADITIONS ARE
_____
_____
_____
_____
_____
_____

Summertime Fun

MY FAVORITE SUMMER MEMORIES ARE _____

_____

_____

_____

_____

_____

_____

_____

_____

MY FAVORITE HOBBIES DURING SUMMER _____

_____

_____

_____

_____

_____

_____

It's Time For Fall

EVERY YEAR WE CELEBRATE FALL BY

_____

_____

_____

_____

_____

_____

MY FAVORITE FAMILY MEMORY ABOUT THE FALL SEASON IS

_____

_____

_____

_____

_____

LISTEN! THE WIND IS RISING,
AND THE AIR IS WILD WITH LEAVES
WE HAVE HAD OUR SUMMER EVENINGS,
NOW FOR OCTOBER EVE!

WINTER WONDERS

MY FAVORITE WINTER HOLIDAYS ARE

_____

_____

_____

_____

_____

_____

TRADITIONAL GATHERINGS THAT BRING US ALL TOGETHER

_____

_____

_____

_____

_____

_____

_____

_____

HOLIDAY
PHOTOGRAPH

HOLIDAY
PHOTOGRAPH

It's Time for Vacation!

THE BEST FAMILY VACATION WE'VE TAKEN WAS _____

_____

_____

_____

_____

WE HAVE HAD SO MUCH FUN VISITING OUR RELATIVES IN _____

_____

_____

_____

_____

SOME OF MY FAVORITE STORIES ABOUT OUR FAMILY VACATIONS

_____

_____

_____

_____

_____

_____

_____

My Family Traditions

AS A FAMILY, WE CELEBRATE _____

_____

_____

_____

_____

SOME OF MY FAVORITE FAMILY TRADITIONS ARE _____

_____

_____

_____

_____

SOME TRADITIONS THAT HAVE BEEN PASSED DOWN THROUGH SEVERAL

GENERATIONS ARE _____

_____

_____

_____

_____

HOME SWEET HOME

MY FIRST ADDRESS WAS

THIS IS A LITTLE BIT ABOUT MY FIRST HOME

A LITTLE SOMETHING ABOUT MY NEIGHBORHOOD

WE LIVED HERE FOR

MY FAVORITE NEIGHBORS THAT LIVED ON MY BLOCK

MY FAVORITE PLACES WHERE I PLAYED WERE

I REMEMBER STORIES ABOUT FAMILY HOMES

WE HAD MANY FAMILY ACTIVITIES IN OUR HOUSE

THIS IS A STORY ABOUT MY BEST FRIEND AND I GROWING UP

Family Heritage

MY FAMILY CAME TO THIS COUNTRY BY _____

_____

_____

_____

_____

_____

MY FAMILY SETTLED IN THIS COUNTRY AND BEGAN OUR HISTORY IN _____

_____

_____

_____

THESE ARE SPECIAL FAMILY CUSTOMS THAT HAVE LIVED THROUGH GENERATIONS

_____

_____

_____

_____

_____

_____

STICKS IN A BUNDLE
ARE UNBREAKABLE. - KENYAN PROVERB

FAMILY
PHOTOGRAPH

FAMILY
PHOTOGRAPH

My Famous Family

WE HAVE A FAMOUS PERSON IN OUR FAMILY. THIS IS WHO THAT

PERSON IS AND WHY THEY ARE FAMOUS.

_____

_____

_____

WE ARE LUCKY TO HAVE A RELATIVE WHO...

_____

_____

_____

_____

THESE ARE ORGANIZATIONS THAT MY FAMILY BELONGS TO

_____

_____

_____

_____

Sing Me a Song

WHEN MY FAMILY GETS TOGETHER WE LIKE TO SING _____

_____

_____

_____

THE LULLABIES AND SONGS THAT WE GREW UP WITH ARE _____

_____

_____

I WOULD LIKE TO PASS THESE SONGS ALONG TO MY FAMILY _____

_____

_____

_____

IF I COULD CHOOSE ANY INSTRUMENT, I WOULD LIKE TO PLAY ____

_____

Fun Time Family Activities

WE LIKE TO GET TOGETHER AND PLAY
_____
_____
_____

THE BOOKS WE LIKE TO READ, SHARE AND ENJOY
_____
_____
_____

WE LIKE TO GATHER AT THESE RESTAURANTS
_____
_____
_____

GAMES THAT WE LIKE TO PLAY TOGETHER
_____
_____

ACTIVITIES WE LIKE TO DO AS A FAMILY
_____
_____

PHOTOGRAPH

PHOTOGRAPH

Food brings us together

MEALTIME IS WHEN WE SIT DOWN AT THE TABLE AND ENJOY

EACH OTHER. HERE IS A SPECIAL STORY ABOUT A SPECIAL FAMILY MEAL.

_____

_____

_____

_____

THE TRADITIONAL COOKS IN MY FAMILY ARE

_____

_____

_____

MY FAVORITE RECIPES THAT I PLAN TO PASS DOWN

_____

_____

_____

WHEN HUNGER GETS INSIDE YOU, NOTHING ELSE CAN. - YORUBA PROVERB

FAVORITE RECIPES

THIS RECIPE IS FROM

_____

_____

_____

_____

_____

_____

_____

_____

_____

_____

_____

_____

THIS RECIPE IS FROM

_____

_____

_____

_____

_____

_____

_____

_____

_____

_____

_____

_____

I WILL COUNT MY BLESSINGS

HAVE EACH FAMILY MEMBER
WRITE A SPECIAL BLESSING

I will count my Blessings

Have each family member
write a special blessing

AVAILABLE RECORD BOOKS FROM HAVOC

A CELEBRATION OF MEMORIES
A CIRCLE OF LOVE
BABY
COLLEGE LIFE
COUPLES
FAMILY
FOREVER FRIENDS
GIRLFRIENDS
GRANDMOTHER
GRANDPARENTS
HEART TO HEART
IT'S ALL ABOUT ME!
MOTHERS & DAUGHTERS
MY PREGNANCY
OUR HONEYMOON
SCHOOL DAYS
SISTERS
TYING THE KNOT

havoc®
PUBLISHING